KEYS TO THE CITY

Walks exploring Newcastle's hidden history

Vanessa Histon

Tyne Bridge Publishing gratefully acknowledges the invaluable assistance of Ian Ayris, Historic Environment Manager; Peter Brennan; David Brookbanks, Theatre Royal; David Heslop, Tyne & Wear County Archaeologist; Rev Terry Hurst; Ian Jackson; Alan Morgan, City Guide; Paul MacDonald, Castle Keep; Lynn Redhead, Holy Jesus Hospital.

Our thanks to Insite Environments, the Landscape and Urban Design Consultants for their generous support. Insite Environments work in a variety of sectors from education and infrastructure, through to housing and regeneration projects and are well known for their innovative application of Virtual Reality to visualise development proposals.

Our thanks also to Blackfriars Restaurant, the oldest purpose-built restaurant in the UK, for their support. Blackfriars Restaurant has won several awards for its gutsy modern British menu including Best Restaurant in the North East from Observer readers.

Photographic acknowledgments: unless otherwise indicated all illustrations are part of the collections of Newcastle Libraries.

The maps were drawn by Katherine Pentney.

ISBN: 978 1 85795 1141

Published by
City of Newcastle upon Tyne
Newcastle Libraries & Information
Service
Tyne Bridge Publishing
2007

Tyne Bridge Publishing
Newcastle Libraries
PO Box 88
Newcastle upon Tyne
NE99 1DX
www.tynebridgepublishing.co.uk

Printed by Elanders Hindson, North Tyneside

Contents

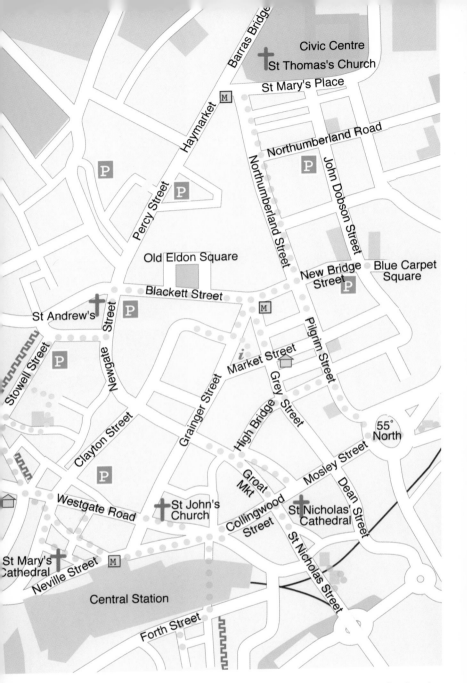

The highlighted streets show the coverage of all five walks in this book, but there is much else to explore in Newcastle.

Call in at the Visitor Information Centres on Market Street, and at the Guildhall on the Quayside to find out more about the city.

Keys to the City

With a long and occasionally turbulent history, the character and even the location of Newcastle's centre has changed over the centuries. In its earliest days the settlement clung to the riverbanks. In later centuries the town's medieval heart grew up on the sandstone bluff above the steep valley of the Tyne, with its Castle Keep, nearby markets, and surrounding defensive walls. The late 18th century saw new streets and buildings add Georgian elegance to the appearance of the growing town. In the 1830s Richard Grainger gave it a new heart, with arteries spreading out from the dominating landmark of the Grey Monument. The rise of Northumberland Street, by the 1930s one of the country's premier shopping streets, confirmed the continued march of the city centre northwards, a trend which was accelerated by the building of the Civic Centre and the growth of the two universities.

In a series of informal walks which follow the meandering history of the town, this guide picks out the places and people which have made the city famous, and points the reader to the locations of many of the city's commemorative plaques. We take you down Northumberland Street, around Grainger Town, along the old Town Walls, into the Heart of the City and the Stephenson Quarter, and revisit Newcastle's different identities through the ages – Norman stronghold, medieval fortress, Georgian showcase, industrial giant, modern metropolis.

Newcastle's history is long and deep, its character complex. It has something for everyone – tranquil corners of Blackfriars, the hurly burly which has returned to the Haymarket area, lively street scenes, new art, and activities in the pavement cafés and open spaces of Grainger Town. *Keys to the City* unlocks all of this and, like the city itself, will give pleasure to curious visitors and proud residents alike. Take the walks, follow the guide, read the plaques and the soul of the city will open up before you.

Ian Ayris, Historic Environment Manager, 2007

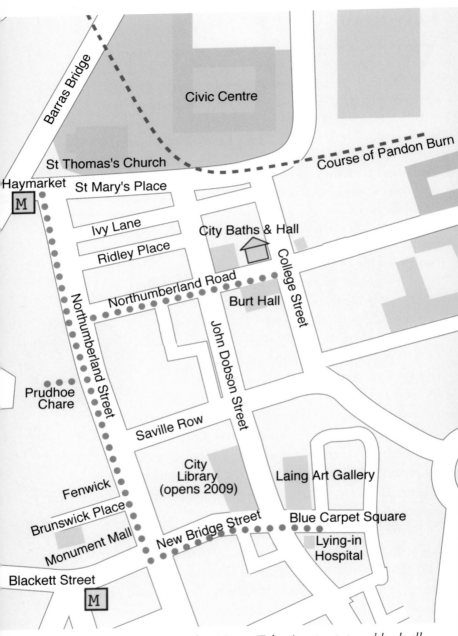

Start your walk at Haymarket Metro. Take time to stop and look all around you. Northumberland Street, Saville Row and Blue Carpet Square are pedestrianised.

Look out for buildings which are part of Newcastle's Commemorative Plaque Scheme, highlighted in blue in the text.

Haymarket to Blue Carpet

Start: Haymarket Metro

It's hard to imagine today, but this area was once one of the most feared parts of Newcastle. In the 12th century it was the site of the hospital of St Mary Magdalene. The location was well away from the main centre of population (which was in the quayside area) because the hospital catered for lepers. No one understood how this terrible and disfiguring disease was spread, so to protect the healthy population lepers were obliged to live well outside the Town Walls. They were cared for by monks and nuns and supported themselves by begging from the pilgrims who were making their way to St Mary's Chapel at Jesmond, where 'divers miracles' had been reported. The leper hospital stood on what is now **St Mary's Place** and the bodies of leprosy victims were buried in the area now covered by **St Thomas's Church**. West of the church, linking Haymarket with the Great North Road, is Barras Bridge, thought to take its name from the burial mounds or barrows that filled the area. As leprosy became less of a threat, the land around Barras Bridge (the attractively named Sickman's Close) was used to bury impoverished victims of plague and other diseases.

Remains of the leper hospital survived until the beginning of the 19th century. As the land was redeveloped vast quantities of human bones were uncovered.

Newcastle's Civic Centre, beyond St Thomas's Church is a fine expression of 1960s architecture with attractive green spaces to explore.

Sam Fairless

At the beginning of the 19th century the Haymarket was just a piece of waste ground. In 1808, when Britain needed soldiers to fight in the Napoleonic wars, the land was paved to create a parade ground for the Newcastle Volunteers.

There wasn't actually a market here until 1824. Then, for over 100 years, hay and straw were sold here every Tuesday. The market was also a hiring fair where people came to meet local farmers who were looking for workers. A venue for open air meetings, the Haymarket had more exotic visitors such as menageries, wax-works, fat women and living skeletons. The market ceased trading in the 1930s when it became a bus station.

The War Memorial which stands here today was erected in around 1907 to commemorate the soldiers who gave their lives in the South African War.

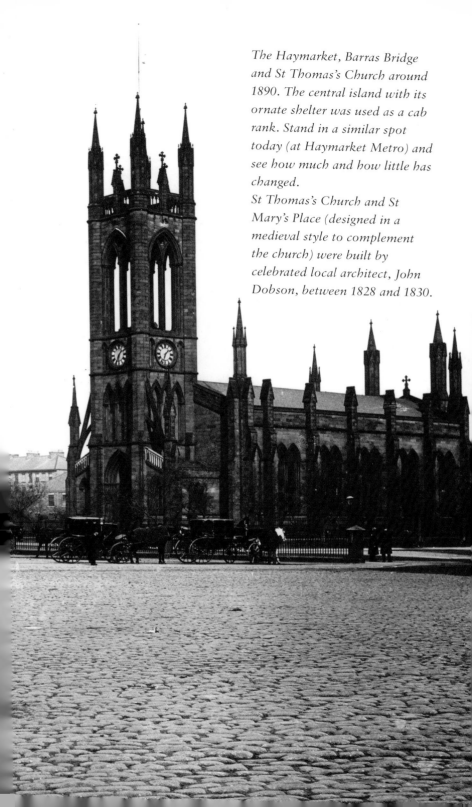

The Haymarket, Barras Bridge and St Thomas's Church around 1890. The central island with its ornate shelter was used as a cab rank. Stand in a similar spot today (at Haymarket Metro) and see how much and how little has changed.

St Thomas's Church and St Mary's Place (designed in a medieval style to complement the church) were built by celebrated local architect, John Dobson, between 1828 and 1830.

Art around the Haymarket

The lofty figure holding a banner outside Haymarket Metro station, and his twin who stands near the Blackett Street junction with Northumberland Street, are *Heralds*, produced by sculptor Ray Smith and installed in 1997 and 1999.

Shoulder to Shoulder (2000), also by Ray Smith, the concrete figures by the South African War Memorial, represent Roman Soldiers carrying spears.

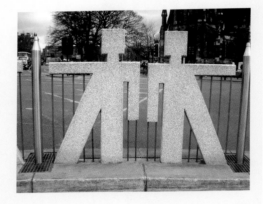

Sam Fairless

Look out for the rather beautiful relief panel on BHS near the top of Northumberland Road depicting Newcastle through the ages. The artists were Henry and Joyce Collins whose work can be seen on the Post Office Tower in London. The style is very representative of the 1960s-1970s.

Northumberland Street was developed during the 18th century as housing for well-to-do townsfolk. Like many streets in Newcastle it is best enjoyed by looking up, above the level of the shop fronts, so you can appreciate the wide diversity of 18th, 19th and 20th century architecture.

The postcard above shows Northumberland Street around 1910. Some of the 18th century houses can still be seen. The postcard below shows the street in around 1913 with Fenwick's new white facade.

John Dobson's Northumberland Road baths in the 1890s.

Below, proud swimmers at the newly opened 'small pool' in the state of the art 1928 baths.

Turn left into Northumberland Road which runs east from Northumberland Street, and walk down to cross John Dobson Street (named for the architect who designed many of Newcastle's 19th century buildings).

On your left are the City Pool and City Hall. Both the pool (still with its original Turkish bath) and the City Hall were opened in 1928. The City Pool was built on the site of earlier public baths, designed by John Dobson and opened in 1839. Although the proposal for Dobson's baths must have seemed attractive (the building was funded by public subscription), the novelty soon wore off and shortly after opening part of the structure was converted into an inn.

A spanking new City Hall and Baths, 1928.

M. Noble

The City Hall is a venue for music and comedy. As well as classical music giants such as Sir Malcolm Sargent, Yehudi Menuhin and Kathleen Ferrier, the hall has hosted shows by rock and pop acts like Little Richard, Jerry Lee Lewis, Bob Dylan, The Beatles, The Rolling Stones, Bruce Springsteen, and Elton John. During the 1960s shows featuring five or six acts were common and local music fans could watch Gerry and the Pacemakers, Gene Pitney, The Kinks and Marianne Faithful on one bill for around ten shillings and sixpence.

Stand at the corner of College Street, look over the road at the statue on the wall of the red brick building opposite. It

represents Dame Eleanor Allan, the daughter of a Newcastle goldsmith and widow of a wealthy tobacco merchant. In 1705 Dame Allan founded schools to provide a proper education for 40 poor boys and 20 poor girls of the city parishes. The College Street building housed the schools from 1882 until they moved to Fenham in the 1930s.

On the opposite side of Northumberland Road is the Sutherland Building, built between 1887 and 1895. It is now part of Northumbria University, but was once the Newcastle Medical School and later the Dental School.

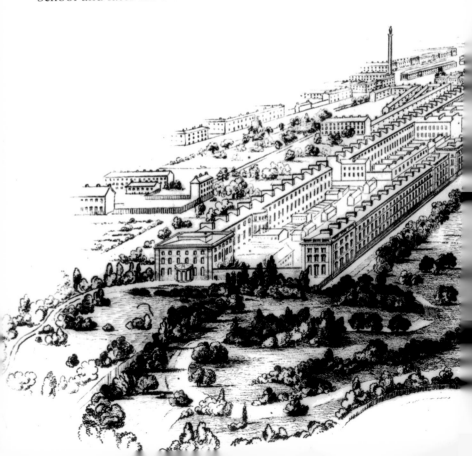

The area around College Street used to be the site of a cricket ground. This was the private ground of Northumberland Cricket Club who moved here from the Town Moor in 1839. They occupied the site until 1881 when the land was sold for building. The most notable match played here was a drawn game in August 1868 against the first Australian team (including ten Aboriginal players) to visit Britain.

The cricket club, baths, and St Thomas's around 1853. The little house was a charity school.

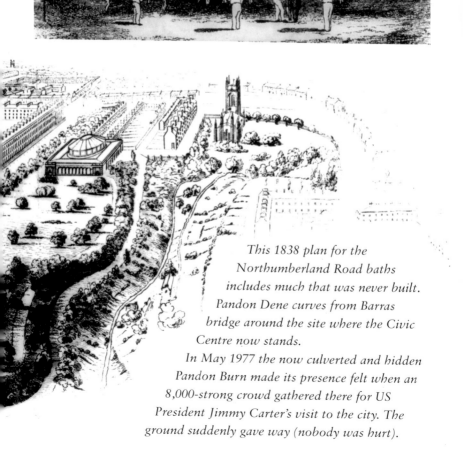

This 1838 plan for the Northumberland Road baths includes much that was never built. Pandon Dene curves from Barras bridge around the site where the Civic Centre now stands.

In May 1977 the now culverted and hidden Pandon Burn made its presence felt when an 8,000-strong crowd gathered there for US President Jimmy Carter's visit to the city. The ground suddenly gave way (nobody was hurt).

Burt Hall, on the south side of Northumberland Road, was built in 1895 as the headquarters of the Northumberland Miners' Association. It was named in honour of Thomas Burt (1837-1922), the first working miner to become an MP. Born at Backworth, near Newcastle, he was a pit lad from the age of ten. Self-educated, he served as the Association's general secretary for 48 years and was MP for Morpeth 1874-1918. A report describing the opening of Burt Hall records: 'The walls are faced with Red Leicestershire bricks, with stone dressings from Brunton and Dunhouse quarries, and part dressings of terra-cotta; the roof is covered with green Westmorland slates. The Northumberland Road front has an oriel window entirely of stone, on the summit of which stands a miner in stone, taken from Mr Ralph Hedley's picture 'Going Home'. In the centre of the gable are the Northumberland county arms.'

The building next to Burt Hall, with its old stone pillars, was a riding school, built by John Dobson in 1847. Both buildings are now part of Northumbria University.

The miner going home

The statue of the miner on top of Burt Hall is based on the younger of two figures in local artist Ralph Hedley's painting Going Home which depicts two miners returning from work. The statue is about seven feet high and stands on a base representing a mound of coal. According to one observer writing in 1895 'There is a contented look in the face of the figure'. Hedley's original painting is part of the collection at the Laing Art Gallery.

Northumberland Road around 1912 was full of leisure opportunities. White City, beyond the Olympia, housed the Dreamland Ballroom de Luxe. Later, as a theatre, it boasted a water tank that could hold 30,000 gallons for the 'latest aquatic shows'. It had begun life as an ice rink.

Northumberland Road was the venue for what was probably the first beauty contest in the UK. In December 1905, The Olympia (a hall which staged both variety and early moving picture shows) played host to *The Blonde and Brunette Beauty Show*. Sadly, no record of the contestants seems to have survived. The Olympia was destroyed by fire in December 1907, though the above photo suggests some repairs. A second Olympia was built next door in 1910. That building closed as a cinema in 1961 and was demolished in 1971 to make way for John Dobson Street.

Turn left into Northumberland Street and glance into Prudhoe Chare to your right between Marks and

Spencer and Eldon Square. On the wall are sculpted details reclaimed from various old Newcastle buildings. The heads include Thomas Bewick the engraver, George Stephenson the railway pioneer (right), and Admiral Collingwood. The seahorse is part of Newcastle's crest.

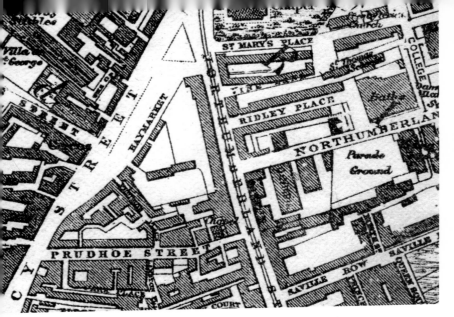

The Northumberland Street area in 1899.

Widow Green's flower show

Before the Eldon Square shopping centre was built, Prudhoe Chare was once Prudhoe Street, and linked Northumberland Street and Percy Street. Around 250 years ago a flower show was hosted by 'Widow Green' at her house in

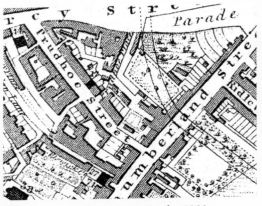

A greener Prudhoe Street in the 1830s.

Northumberland Street. John Wesley records in his diary that the visitors had dinner in a marquee, specially erected on the bowling green which stood in the area that is now Prudhoe Chare. By 1889 the bowling green and the gardens and orchards around it had long been swept away, and Prudhoe Street was described as having 'a huge public-house at either end and five establishments of the same sort between; a pawnshop and a police station; and some squalid alleys'.

These lovely windows upstairs on your right just after the entrance to Eldon Square graced Summerfield the jewellers who traded here for over 60 years.

Over the road you will see a fine Victorian building among the modern shop fronts. There is a huge variety of periods and styles to be seen.

HARRY HOTSPUR

ROGER THORNTON

Gradually the focus of Northumberland Street changed from the private housing of the 18th century to a flourishing retail centre. By the early 1930s, it was claimed to be the most important British shopping street outside London.

A little further down the street, on your left, is a cream-painted building featuring four niches, each holding a statue of a local worthy. They are:

Sir Henry Percy (1366-1403), who, because of his ferocity in combat, was known as Harry Hotspur. He earned his reputation (and a place in Shakespearian literature) in several campaigns against the Scots.

Roger Thornton (died about 1429) rose from rags to riches, making an immense fortune as a merchant as well as becoming Newcastle's mayor and an MP.

Sir John Marley (1590-1673) defended Newcastle against the

besieging Scottish army in 1644. After the Civil War and the Restoration, he served as Newcastle's mayor on several occasions.

Thomas Bewick (1755-1828) was an internationally renowned artist and wood engraver who spent most of his working life in Newcastle. The portrait is no great likeness however! See page 65.

The building was designed for Boots the Chemists and opened in 1912. The sculptor is unknown.

Nearby is a plaque marking the site of the **Orphan House** which was built by John Wesley in about 1743. Despite its name, the building was never used as an orphanage, but became the headquarters of Methodism in the North. As well as a chapel and meeting rooms, the Orphan House provided accommodation for preachers and their families. Wesley, who was a frequent visitor to Newcastle, had a tiny study (apparently just 11 feet square) in the roof space. After preaching at the Orphan House, John Wesley recorded in his diary on 21 April 1751: 'The spirit of the

people refreshed me much, as it almost always does. I wish all our societies were like-minded – as loving, simple and zealous of good works'.

The building was replaced by a Wesleyan School in 1857. The school was demolished in 1955.

Wesley's Newcastle

John Wesley visited the town many times, and, after a bad first impression, became very fond of the place.

Describing his first visit in May 1742 he said: 'We came to Newcastle about six, and, after a short refreshment, walked into the town. I was surprised; so much drunkenness, cursing, and swearing (even from the mouths of little children) do I never remember to have seen and heard before, in so small a compass of time.'

Things soon improved. Commenting on the effects of his

Wesley's Orphan House, Northumberland Street, around the time it was built, 1743.

preaching in a letter to the Mayor of Newcastle on 12 July 1743, Wesley wrote: 'The drunkards are sober, the common swearers fear God, the Sabbath-breakers now keep that day holy.'

In a journal entry of 4 June 1759, Wesley describes how attached he has become to the town: 'I rode to Newcastle. Certainly if I did not believe there was another world, I should spend all my summers here, as I know no place in Great Britain comparable to it for pleasantness.'

Fenwick attracts the crowds to its summer sale in 1898.

Fenwick is one of Newcastle's oldest family businesses. In 1882, Mr J. J. Fenwick opened a shop at 5 Northumberland Street. With his two assistants he provided exclusive tailoring for ladies. The business grew quickly and in 1885 when two houses became available at 37 and 39 Northumberland Street, Mr Fenwick lost no time in converting them into new premises for his store. The splendid new shop caused something of a sensation; there was a large metal statue in the entrance and the frames of

BOND STREET

TAILORING

Fenwick advertises in The Tatler, 1928.

the display windows were decorated in gold leaf. Five years later Fenwick opened the Bijou Tea Room (said to be one of the first cafes in Newcastle) and Mr Fenwick's son, Mr Fred, joined the family firm. Mr Fred was fortunate enough to be sent to Paris to study retail businesses there and came back determined to pursue a fashion that was taking the French capital by storm – the department store. It took a while for Mr Fenwick to accept Mr Fred's new-fangled ideas, but in November 1902 the store proudly advertised:

> *A welcome to customers to walk around the store.*
> *Assistants are not allowed to speak to visitors.*
> *Walk round today, don't buy.*
> *There is time for that another day.*

At a time when most shops kept their goods safely tucked behind a counter and it was the assistant's job to persuade the customer to buy, this was quite revolutionary.

Over the years Fenwick expanded by taking over adjacent buildings. The current Northumberland Street shop front dates from 1913. Around the corner on Blackett

The birth of the trilby hat

Fenwick's Bond Street venture was assisted by publicity gained from the stage production of George Du Maurier's Trilby. In recognition of the heroine, Dorothea Baird (later Mrs Henry Irving), having been born on the site of the Newcastle shop, Fenwick made her gown, costume and soft felt hat complete with narrow brim and indented crown. The birth of the trilby hat was complete!

Street is another entrance to the store dating from 1937. From its Newcastle beginnings, Fenwick established a presence in other British cities including a store in London's Bond Street.

As you pass Fenwick's south entrance on Northumberland Street, look down the alley to Brunswick Chapel which dates from 1821.

On the east of Northumberland Street there is a building that looks almost Elizabethan because of the ornate plasterwork (known as pargetting) on the upper storey. Although it's actually a 19th century building, the decoration is Elizabethan, but from the time of Elizabeth II rather than Elizabeth I. The plasterwork was applied to celebrate her coronation in 1953.

Now turn left into New Bridge Street.

Crowds on Northumberland Street for Queen Elizabeth's visit, 1954. The newly pargetted building is on the right.

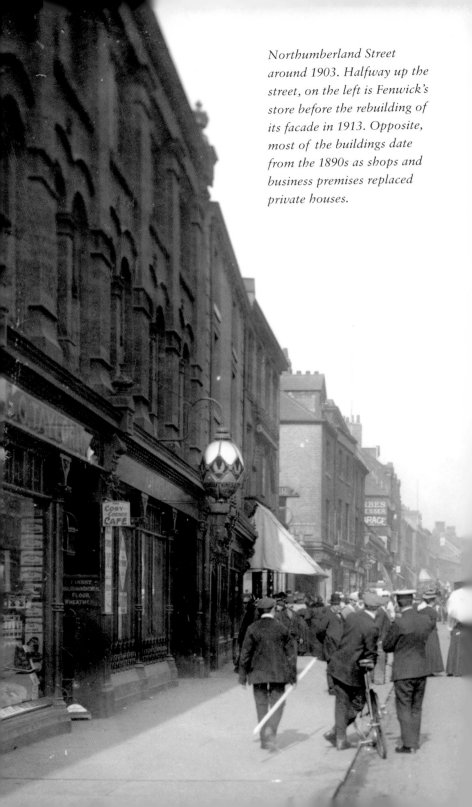

Northumberland Street around 1903. Halfway up the street, on the left is Fenwick's store before the rebuilding of its facade in 1913. Opposite, most of the buildings date from the 1890s as shops and business premises replaced private houses.

Electric trams were introduced from 1901 and were very popular.
By the time of this photograph around 169 trams were in service and soon tracks were laid throughout the city.
They were much more frequent and reliable than the old horse trams. And much cleaner!

Women on the march

Northumberland Street was always a popular street for marches and demonstrations. Below, a rather modest group of suffragettes advertise a particularly relevant issue of their magazine in 1912.

A cunning but deadly plan

Northumberland Court was a little street of tenements which stood where Monument Mall is now, at the bottom of Northumberland Street. In the early 1850s a man called William Glover lived in an upstairs room in one of these old houses. He suspected money was being  pilfered from his room so he devised a cunning plan. He got hold of a 'horse' pistol, loaded it with slugs, and attached it to the door so that anyone breaking in would set it off. He could open the door safely himself by pulling on a string first. Unfortunately on the evening of 6 December 1852 he came home rather the worse for wear and forgot to pull the string. He died from a good mix of paranoia and stupidity.

Northumberland Street in 1987 at the switching on of the Christmas lights by the Mayor of Bergen. Though the days when Northumberland Street was part of the A1 north were long past, traffic was still jostling for space with pedestrians.

The mystery of the hidden streams

Several of Newcastle's streets have the word 'bridge' in their names (Barras Bridge, New Bridge Street, High Bridge and Low Bridge), but there is no sign of water near any of them. In medieval times Newcastle was divided by a number of streams and burns which ran into the Tyne. The street names indicate where the bridges that crossed these waterways used to be. As the town expanded over the centuries, the rivers made getting around more difficult so they were filled in. They still flow through Newcastle today, but deep beneath the city's streets.

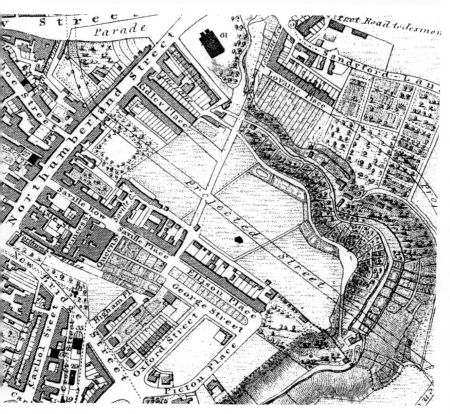

This 1830s map shows the deep valley of the Pandon Burn (right). New Bridge Street leads to a bridge across this stream. Today the Erick Burn flows beneath the Laing Art Gallery to join the now culverted Pandon Burn nearer the Tyne. The Lort Burn flows beneath today's Grey Street.

Cross John Dobson Street to the Laing Art Gallery.

The Laing Art Gallery dates from 1904 and was founded by Alexander Laing, a Scottish wine and spirit merchant. It houses an extensive collection of British oil paintings including *Isabella and the Pot of Basil* by William Holman Hunt, *Laus Veneris* by Edward Coley Burne Jones, *The Lovers* by Stanley Spencer and and an important group of works by John Martin (who was born at Haydon Bridge). There are also works by Auerbach, Nicholson, Hitchen, Bomberg and Moore and watercolours by J.M.W. Turner and Edward Lear. Important decorative art collections include Beilby enamelled glass, Newcastle silver, North East pottery, early 19th century creamwares and 19th and 20th earthenwares by Maling pottery.

In front of the Laing is Blue Carpet Square, designed by Thomas Heatherwick in 2001. The tiles are made from recycled blue glass set in resin.

An avant garde opening

When the Laing was built it did not possess a collection as its benefactor had not been a collector or a connoisseur. At its opening there were no works of art to exhibit, so to highlight its plight the empty gallery opened with only wood shavings from the construction on display! The situation soon improved.

Mark Pinder

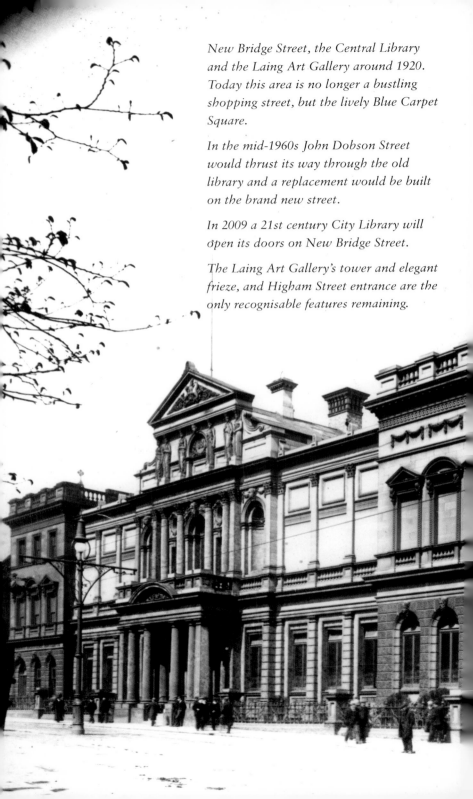

New Bridge Street, the Central Library and the Laing Art Gallery around 1920. Today this area is no longer a bustling shopping street, but the lively Blue Carpet Square.

In the mid-1960s John Dobson Street would thrust its way through the old library and a replacement would be built on the brand new street.

In 2009 a 21st century City Library will open its doors on New Bridge Street.

The Laing Art Gallery's tower and elegant frieze, and Higham Street entrance are the only recognisable features remaining.

To the east of the art gallery is a nightclub. Originally this was the home of John Dobson, the celebrated local architect, built to his own design in 1823. There was a long garden at the rear where Dobson kept his collection of architectural fragments.

Dobson was born in North Shields and educated in London. He brought fashionable ideas from London back to the North East where he had an immensely successful career designing grand country houses, imposing terraces and crescents, churches, railway stations, hospitals, schools and even prisons. His work can be seen all over Newcastle and the North East.

After John Dobson's time his house was bought by Henry Donnelly, who ran it as a lodging house. Donnelly, who had other lodging houses in Newcastle, was obviously not a very conscientious landlord because he inspired a Geordie expression used to describe anywhere that was in a mess: 'just like Donnelly's lodging houses'. Subsequently Dobson's house has had various incarnations as a nightspot, including the Oxford Galleries, an immensely popular ballroom in the 1950s and 1960s.

Malcolm Maybury

John Dobson's house (the square building to the left) in the mid 1990s.

34

The Lying-In Hospital in 1820. John Dobson would have been able to see it from his own elegant home on the other side of the street.

Opposite Dobson's house on the south side of New Bridge Street is a gothic style building which was once the **Lying-In Hospital**. In the early 19th century many mothers and babies died in childbirth due to lack of medical knowledge and poor living conditions. The Lying-In Hospital (designed by John Dobson and opened in 1825) was built by charitable subscription to provide better accommodation for mothers giving birth. Each woman who was admitted had to produce her marriage certificate and a child's dress. Unmarried women, the homeless, and those suffering from contagious diseases were turned away. The hospital was used until 1923, by which time it was dreadfully overcrowded and unhygienic, with large cracks in the walls. The building was taken over by the BBC and, in 1925, was officially opened as Broadcasting House. Radio and (eventually) TV programmes were made here until 1988 when the BBC moved to purpose-built studios in Fenham.

Retrace your steps to Northumberland Street.

If you would like to extend your walk, continue into Blackett Street for Grainger and Grey, or head south down Pilgrim Street for Pilgrims and Friars (see page 95).

Start your walk at Monument Metro.
Look out for buildings which are part of Newcastle's Commemorative
Plaque Scheme, highlighted in blue in the text.

Grainger and Grey

Start: Monument Metro: Blackett Street entrance

During the first 20 years of the 19th century, this street was simply a muddy track surrounded by pigsties, manure heaps and rubbish dumps. By 1824, however it had been transformed into a street of elegant new houses, thanks to the vision of Richard Grainger, a local builder. Grainger began his life in humble circumstances. He was born in High Friar Lane, Newcastle, in 1797, the son of a porter. In 1816 he set up a building business with his brother. After building several elegant streets including Higham Place, Blackett Street and Eldon Square, at the age of 37 he embarked on an ambitious plan for the redevelopment of the town centre and completed it within seven years. With the support of John

Blackett Street before 1900. The elegant building to the rear of the picture was the YMCA. It is now an entrance to Eldon Square shopping centre. Much of the view is still the same.

Clayton, the Town Clerk and a team of architects including John Dobson (see page 34) he produced streets of shops and houses in the classical style, including Grey Street and Grainger Street, as well as a theatre and a covered market. The whole area is now known as Grainger Town.

Blackett Street was named after John Erasmus Blackett who was mayor of Newcastle on four occasions during the 18th century.

Before you leave the Metro, take a look at the designs sand blasted into the walls and paving at the entrances to the Metro station. This is *Circuit*, an art work by Richard Cole which was installed in 2002. The work uses the imagery of electronic circuit boards to explore our modern-day digital culture which relies on circuits and networks like the Metro, activated by information and people.

Now cross Blackett Street to Grey's Monument.

Charles, 2nd Earl Grey, was Prime Minister from 1830 to 1834. He supported the Reform Act of 1832 ('to prevent the necessity of revolution') which swept away many anomalies in the electoral system and extended the vote to men who occupied property with an annual value of £10 (in effect this meant that around one adult male in seven had the right to vote). In 1836, some of Grey's friends and admirers started a public subscription for a monument to celebrate Grey's achievement. The scheme wasn't very popular; it took a long time to raise funds for construction and even Grey himself was absent from the stone laying and completion ceremonies. Architects John and Benjamin Green designed a column topped with a statue of Grey (twice life size), sculpted by Edward Hodges Baily (who also sculpted Nelson for Trafalgar Square). Column, plinth and statue total 156ft. Work was completed in August 1838, and the street formerly known as Upper Dean Street was renamed Grey Street. Beneath the monument is buried a glass vessel containing the original plans, a list of subscribers, and a collection of gold and silver coins and medals donated by former mayor John Fenwick.

Earl Grey lost his head in 1941 when it was struck off by lightning (amazingly nobody was injured)! A new head was sculpted by Roger Hedley (son of artist Ralph Hedley) in 1947.

Set into the plinth of the Monument are glass cubes, each containing an image of the head of Earl Grey viewed from a different angle. Artist Simon Watkinson used a casting of Grey's head taken while the monument was being cleaned to make a pattern for the heads. *Head Cubes* was installed in 2002.

Stan Gamster

Earl Grey's tea time

According to tradition Earl Grey Tea was specially blended by a Chinese mandarin for Charles, 2nd Earl Grey to suit the water at the family seat at Howick, near Craster, Northumberland. The Howick water has a high lime content, so bergamot was added to the tea to offset the taste.

A view down the elegant Grey and Grainger Streets, 1885.

Now walk a little way along Grey Street to the Waterstone's building. Officially known as Royal Exchange Buildings, this was formerly the premises of Mawson, Swan and Morgan, booksellers and art dealers. Mawson, Swan and Morgan had the only shop in the city with its own private street lighting. This is, perhaps, unusual but understandable when you realise that the

Mawson Swan & Morgan, now Waterstone's, decorated for the 1953 coronation of Elizabeth II. It was refronted in 1904.

Swan part of the partnership was Joseph Swan (1828-1914) inventor of the carbon filament incandescent lamp. Swan worked with chemist and druggist, John Mawson, at his first shop on Mosley Street. From the 1840s Swan began experimenting with electric lighting in a laboratory above the shop. In 1880 Mosley Street became the first street in the UK to be lit by electric light. In 1883 the Edison and Swan United Electric Light Company was established. Swan produced many other inventions including several important photographic processes. The Grey Street shop, with its ornate cast iron street lamps, was redeveloped in the Italian style for Mawson Swan & Morgan in 1904.

During the 13th century the Franciscan, or Grey, friars built a friary in this part of Newcastle. In the middle of the 16th century many religious buildings were closed and sold off by Henry VIII. A wealthy Newcastle merchant, Robert Anderson, acquired the land in 1580 and built a fine house (roughly on the site of the Lloyds TSB bank) with extensive grounds. It was known as the 'Newe House'. In 1646, King Charles I, who had been captured by the Scots, was imprisoned here for about 10 months. The property passed to the Blackett family in 1675. Writing in 1736, historian Henry Bourne describes the house: 'surrounded with a vast quantity of ground: that part of it which faces the street is thrown into walks and grass-plots, beautified and beset with trees, which afford a very pleasing shade: the other parts of the ground on the west side of it is all a garden, exceedingly neat and curious, adorned with many and the most beautiful statues, and several other curiosities'.

In 1782 the house was bought by George Anderson (no relation to the first owner), a wealthy local builder. He was followed, in 1801, by his son, Major Anderson, who changed the name of the house to Anderson Place. In 1827, historian Eneas McKenzie wrote of 'a grand and noble mansion … [with] some curious and well-painted ceilings.' Major Anderson died in 1831 and this beautiful house, along with its neat and curious gardens, was sold in 1833 for £50,000 to Richard Grainger to make way for his ambitious redevelopments.

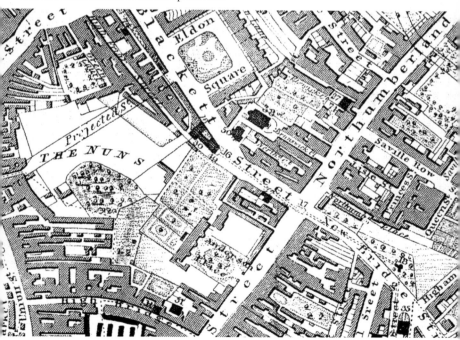

In this 1830 map the gardens of Anderson Place (centre) cover the site Grey Street and Grey's Monument. The Nuns marks the site of the old St Bartholomew's nunnery. Richard Grainger's masterplan was about to change the face of the town.

*The magnificent Tyneside Classical sweep of Grey Street was
completed in 1837 by John Dobson and other architects.*

*Insite Environments designed street furniture (seats, bins and
bicycle racks) for Grainger Town in 2003. They brought together glass*

designer Cate Watkinson and writer Julia Darling to create the
imaginative seating. Nine of the seats depict 'nine things to do on a
bench' etched into glass backrests. The granite benches (this one is
outside the Theatre Royal) are illuminated by LED lighting at night.

Continue down Grey Street to the Theatre Royal. This elegant theatre was designed by architects John and Benjamin Green and opened in February 1837. The first performance was a double bill: *The Merchant of Venice* and *The Young Widow*. According to T. Sopwith, in an 1838 guide book to Newcastle, £1,000 was spent on decorating the theatre, though there must have been some economies because:

'A considerable portion of the new scenery was painted by the manager, Mr. Penley … The painting and perspective of the scenery is admirably done: the drop-scene represents the Temple of Jupiter in the Aegina. The depth of 22 feet under the stage and numerous other arrangements admit a greater variety scenic effects and transformations being accomplished than in any other theatre in the kingdom, Drury Lane and Convent [sic] Garden only excepted. The machinery for scenes is also very complete.'

Despite considerable investment in all the latest theatrical technology, Mr Sopwith was forced to admit: 'The attendance generally is tolerably good.'

Sopwith also wrote: 'The corridors surrounding the pit and boxes are built of stone and consequently fire proof.'

Unfortunately this claim was untrue, as, in 1899, fire completely destroyed the inside of the building. The present Edwardian interior was designed by Frank Matcham in 1901, with further remodelling in 1987 and 2006.

This is a splendid place to view the majestic sweep of the lower part of Grey Street, which has been awarded the title Best Street in Britain. In 1838, with not all the buildings completed, it was no less

Grey Street has been awarded the title Best Street in Britain – its lovely curve is seen here in a painting by artist Phil R. Daniels for the Theatre Royal's safety curtain. (Theatre Royal)

well thought of. In Sopwith's opinion:

'Grey Street stands unequalled in the world as a street built merely for business. In richness and variety of architecture it exceeds Regent Street, and has the great advantage over it of being built of solid stone instead of brick faced with stucco. The business streets of Edinburgh, though built of stone, are plain, monotonous and sombre when compared with the sumptuous and palace-like aspect of Grey Street.

'On reaching the head of Dean Street, it bursts on the view more like a fairy enchantment than a substantial reality.'

Retrace your steps to the crossroad and turn left along Market Street. The building on the corner above the coffee shop was Coxon's, a popular high-class store from the 1840s until 1928.

Coxon's, in the 1920s, not long before its demise. If you look at the building now you will see that the top layer of dormitory windows has vanished.

Dormitories high in the roof housed members of staff (who came from as far away as Bishop Auckland). The building also housed an official ferret keeper to keep down the rats!

Call at the Visitor Information Centre on the north side of Market Street (there is another at the Guildhall on the Quayside), where you will find maps, guides and information. Now turn right into the Central Arcade.

Richard Grainger intended the inside of the Central Exchange Buildings (opened in 1839) to accommodate a corn exchange, but the city fathers had other ideas, so he launched it

as a news room instead. At various stages in its lifetime it has housed a concert hall, art gallery, theatre and 50-bedroom hotel. In 1901 the building was gutted by fire. The interior reopened in 1906, as the Central Arcade, magnificently decorated with a mosaic floor and the glistening Burmantoft's ceramic tiles which are still in place today.

Walk towards the centre of the arcade and leave by the exit on your left. Set into the pavement here is *Grainger Dedication*, an artwork by Charlie Holmes and Ian Ness. The huge cast iron plaque was installed in 2002 and is a monument to Richard Grainger.

Cross Grainger Street and go into Nelson Street.

Can you spot the white plaque on the building at the left hand corner of **Nelson Street**? It commemorates visits to Newcastle by William Lloyd Garrison, American anti-slavery campaigner, in 1876, Louis (born Lajos) Kossuth, Hungarian patriot and statesman, who tried unsuccessfully to establish an independent Hungarian republic, in 1865 and Giuseppe Garibaldi, Italian Nationalist revolutionary in 1854.

A revolutionary visitor

In 1854 Garibaldi was returning to Italy from America on a ship called the *Commonwealth*. He called in at Newcastle to pick up a cargo of coal bound for Genoa. Joseph Cowen, a rich Newcastle newspaper proprietor (who also owned a brick factory), started a collection to present Garibaldi with a sword as an expression of support for the general and his cause. Subscriptions were set at one penny so even working men could afford to contribute, and the appeal was so popular that it raised enough to buy not only a sword (priced £410s) but also a two-guinea telescope. Cowen also gave Garibaldi support of a more practical nature; he is said to have smuggled guns concealed in cargoes of bricks bound for Italy.

Further up on the opposite side of Nelson Street there is a plaque marking the site of the **Music Hall and Lecture Room**, built as part of the Grainger development in 1838. Probably the most famous person to appear here was writer Charles Dickens. He made six visits to Newcastle between 1852 and 1867. On his first visit, Dickens was managing a touring company of players. He acted in two plays: *Not So Bad As We Seem* and *Mr Nightingale's Diary*, which were presented at Newcastle's Old Assembly Rooms. Apparently 600 people paid 12s 6d each to sit in some discomfort in a room built to hold 300. Dickens was immensely popular – perhaps the 19th century equivalent of a rock star – and his public readings from his own works drew large crowds. Dickens liked his Newcastle audience. He wrote: 'A finer audience there is not in England, and I suppose them to be a specially earnest people; for while they can laugh till they shake the roof, they have a very unusual sympathy with what is pathetic or passionate.'

MR CHARLES DICKENS' READINGS.—This eminent novelist gave the first of three readings, in the Music Hall, Nelson-street, last evening. The hall was filled by a most respectable company ; who were gratified with the exquisite treat of hearing *David Copperfield* read (as perhaps no other man living could read it) by its author. It would be superfluous to say one word in praise either of the work or the reader ; and we shall simply advise every one who can possibly make it convenient, not to omit availing himself of one of the two opportunities of enjoying a similar treat, which will be offered to-night and to-morrow night. To-night, Mr Dickens will read Nicholas Nickleby at Mr Squeers' School, and the trial from Pickwick ; and on Saturday night, Little Dombey, and the trial from Pickwick.

LITERARY AND PHILOSOPHICAL SOCIETY.—The com-

Newcastle Courant records Dickens' visit in 1861.

A literary affair

Charles Dickens has another connection with Newcastle. His long-term mistress, actress Nelly Ternan, had lived in the town, on Pilgrim Street, with her family. When she was a baby her father managed the Theatre Royal. The theatrical family often returned to perform in Newcastle where they were very popular.

Go into the **Grainger Market** through a Nelson Street entrance (its plaque is round the corner on Clayton Street). The market was designed by John Dobson for Richard Grainger in 1835. So powerful was Grainger's vision that he had no hesitation in demolishing a relatively recently-built (1808) butcher market to build a replacement that fitted in with his great plan. Perhaps it was worth it. Mr Sopwith's guide book of 1838 declares with passion:

'The Markets are superior in extent, convenience, and elegance, to any in Great Britain. Count St Alegonde, a general in the Russian service and one of the Emperor of Russia's aides-de-camp, stated to the author that in his travels through the whole of

The grand dinner to celebrate the opening of the market, 24 October 1835. Richard Grainger and John Dobson were present. This painting by Henry Perlee Parker is in the Laing Art Gallery. (Tyne & Wear Museums)

Europe and a great portion of Asia, he had not met with any structure, as a market, at all comparable to it.

'The market comprises two parts, the Butchers' Market and the Green Market. The Green Market, when viewed in perspective from either end, presents rather the grandeur of a cathedral than the mere carpentry of a market place ... two handsome stone fountains are placed in the midst of the market.'

After looking round the market, leave by a Nelson Street exit and retrace your steps to the Monument. Now turn left onto Blackett Street.

As you pass, stop for a moment to admire the eccentric architecture of the other Waterstone's Building, Emerson Chambers, which was designed by Benjamin Simpson around 1903.

The red brick hexagonal structure near the entrance to Fenwick's is *Parsons Polygon*. The sculpture, by David Hamilton, was installed in 1985. It commemorates Charles Algernon Parsons whose work on steam turbines (particularly the steam turbine-powered ship *Turbinia*) revolutionised the modern world. The designs pressed into the terracotta cladding of the polygon are abstracted from Parsons' engineering drawings. The polygon is not simply a statue, however. It is essentially a ventilation shaft for the Metro station below.

Emerson Chambers, Blackett Street.

(Sam Fairless)

Continue to **Old Eldon Square**, which was built by Richard Grainger between 1825 and 1831 (the plaque is on no. 1). At the time it was acknowledged as Newcastle's most graceful development and was home to gentlemen and professionals such as doctors and solicitors. Can you spot the building with the blacked out windows? That, too, is part of the Metro's ventilation system.

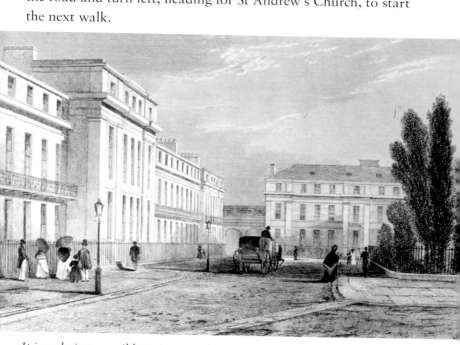

What is it?
Parsons Polygon

Much of the square was demolished in the 1970s to make way for the Eldon Square shopping centre. The statue (by Charles Leonard Hartwell) in the centre of the square is a First World War Memorial, which represents St George and the Dragon.

End your walk here or continue down Blackett Street, cross the road and turn left, heading for St Andrew's Church, to start the next walk.

It is only just possible to imagine how peaceful and elegant Richard Grainger's Eldon Square looked when it was newly built.

Start your walk at St Andrew's Church, Newgate Street.
Look out for buildings which are part of Newcastle's Commemorative
Plaque Scheme, highlighted in blue in the text.

Right, the area of Newgate Street outside St Andrew's was used as a
green market for many years.

Walls and Towers

Start: St Andrew's Church, Newgate Street

St Andrew's church is one of Newcastle's four original parish churches. Some of the masonry dates back to the 12th century and it first appears in records in 1218. Some of the stones used in its construction were taken from the Roman Wall. It has a leper's squint, presumably so lepers from the hospital of St Mary Magdalene at Barras Bridge could watch services without infecting the rest of the congregation.

The tower was added to the church early in the 13th century. In 1280 the **Town Wall** was built over part of the churchyard. Both of these structures saw enemy action during the Civil War. The tower was used as a gun platform and the section of wall near the church was bombarded (though not breached) by the besieging Scots. The church was so badly damaged that, according to parish records of 1645, no children were baptised nor sermons preached for a year.

In 1650 fifteen people who had been executed for witchcraft were buried at St Andrew's. Their neighbours in the churchyard include **Charles Avison** (1709-1770), arguably the most important English composer of concertos in the 18th century and Ralph Beilby (1743-1817), silversmith, jeweller and engraver, who took on Thomas Bewick (see page 66) as an apprentice and later a partner.

Opposite the church is the Art Deco Co-op building, completed in 1933. By the 1930s the Newcastle Co-operative Society was a huge enterprise which had grown from very modest beginnings. Newcastle's first Co-op opened in a tiny shop in Nelson Street in 1861. It traded in the evenings only (because the eleven founder members all had other jobs) to sell flour and groceries. On opening day the entire stock was worth the sum of £17 7s 7½d. After a year the shop was making enough money to employ a full-time sales assistant on £1 4s a week.

Walk up St Andrew's Street (its former name, Darn Crook, probably describes a street that was dark and twisted). At the top of the street there is a view of St James's Park, home of Newcastle United Football Club, through the Chinese arch.

The arch was designed by Mr Yonglai Zhang and constructed

Newcastle's football palace, St James's Park from the Chinese arch on St Andrew's Street.

by a team of twelve traditional craftsmen from Changsu, in the Jiangsu Province. The arch is decorated with carved dragons, phoenixes and other animals. Each side of the arch has seven panels, carved or painted with typical scenes or figures

Look out for the interesting architecture of the Co-op buildings.

from Tyneside. The two stone lions guarding the base of the arch are intended to attract good luck and prosperity to the area.

Now turn along Stowell Street. Look at the gable end on the brick building next to the pub. The Wheatsheaf and the motto 'Labour and Wait' were symbols of the Co-operative wholesale society. This was the Co-op's greengrocery warehouse.

Stowell Street is the heart of Newcastle's Chinese community. Notice that the litter bins, street lighting and other street furniture all have a Chinese theme.

About halfway along Stowell Street, on the right, there are some small brick-built terraced cottages. Dating from around 1824, these are the only survivors of the original Stowell Street, Turn left down the cut opposite these to reach Blackfriars.

Blackfriars was home to the Dominican friars (known as black friars because of their black mantle and cowl) who established a house in Newcastle by around 1239. The friary was abolished by Henry VIII in 1539 and the ten priests and three lay brothers living there were turned out. In 1552 Newcastle Corporation leased the Blackfriars buildings to some of the town's craft guilds (a combination of a trade union and a professional body). The upper floors of the buildings were converted into meeting halls, the lower floors were let out as almshouses for guild members, and eventually the church was demolished. The foundations of the church are exposed in the landscaped area which makes up the fourth (north to catch the best sun) side of what was once the friary's cloister.

Here is Blackfriars around 1790. The medieval friary was long
gone and the buildings were leased to nine trades guilds:
Skinners and Glovers, Tailors, Saddlers, Cordwainers, Butchers,
Tanners, Smiths, Bakers and Brewers, and Fullers and Dyers.

The friars' ground floor refectory (far left) is today, very
appropriately, the award-winning Blackfriars Restaurant. Four of
its windows onto Friars Street are medieval. Upstairs was a
library and the dormitory. The church was on the north side of

the cloister, to catch the sun, but was demolished in the 16th
century. The archaeological excavations show how it was laid
out. The remaining buildings have been altered many times over
the centuries and are now restored. The grassy area was once the
friars' garden where they grew healing herbs, and vegetables.

The curious arch on the wall in the centre of the picture is
still there and was the lavatorium where the friars washed before
eating.

Blackfriars Restaurant

The friars' refectory has now become Blackfriars Restaurant, the oldest purpose-built restaurant in the UK.

Cross the courtyard and exit through the ancient arch on the opposite corner. Turn right into Friars Street and head for the Town Walls which you will see in front of you.

Heber Tower, which stands near the end of Stowell Street, was leased to the Company of Armourers, Curriers and Feltmakers in 1620. By 1831 the company's membership had dwindled to seventeen, and by the end of the 19th century the tower was used as a blacksmith's shop.

The doorway to the Cordwainers' Hall on Friars Street. This was the guild of shoemakers. Nearby is the door to the Blacksmiths' Hall.

Step through the doorway near Heber Tower. The doorway was made in around 1810 to give access to the fever hospital, St Andrew's poor house and the lunatic asylum (both now demolished) which lay outside the walls. The fever hospital, also known as the House of Recovery is the restored three storey stone building which you can see across the car park. It was built in 1804 to isolate poor people suffering from typhus, cholera and smallpox. The hospital closed in 1888 and is now home of Museums, Libraries and Archives North East.

HOUSE OF RECOVERY.

Heber Tower as a black-smith's shop in 1903.

Walls and towers

Isaac Thompson's map of 1746 shows the Town Wall and towers and many medieval features of Newcastle that can still be seen today, including the Castle Keep, Blackfriars, and the churches of St Nicholas, St John, St Andrew, and All Hallows (later All Saints), Newcastle's four original parish churches.

The Lort Burn tumbles down its valley (or dene) following the path now taken by Grey Street and Dean Street.

The medieval street pattern is preserved today in Pilgrim Street, Newgate Street, Westgate Road, Side, Bigg Market and other thoroughfares.

West Wall towers that can still be seen are identified on the map as:

F Gunner Tower
H Pink Tower
K Durham Tower
L Heber Tower
M Morden Tower
N Ever Tower

Towers were often named for the families that funded their building.

The impressive bulk of Heber Tower and Morden Tower beyond.

Turn to face the walls to get a picture of how the approach to Newcastle must have looked in the middle ages. Further along the wall to your left you can see another tower, **Morden Tower**. This was extended upwards in 1619 to provide a meeting room for the Company of Plumbers, Glaziers and Pewterers. This tower is still in use as a venue for poetry readings. Beyond Morden Tower are the remains of **Ever Tower**, once home to the company of Paviours, Colliers and Carriage Men, and, in the 19th century to an eccentric with the evocative name of Hairy Nanny.

The Town Walls

Newcastle's Town Walls were completed by the mid-14th century. The cost of building was funded by murage (wall tax) and the completed structure stretched for over two miles. The walls were between 15 and 20 feet high and between 7 and 10 feet thick, with 6 main gates, 17 towers and several water gates along the riverside. A lane ran around the inside of the walls and a deep ditch was dug on the outside to help fend off attackers. (The ditch was re-dug outside this western section of wall in the 1980s). In around 1500, 100 men patrolled the walls each night. However as the centuries passed and the threat of border warfare with the Scots receded, Newcastle's Corporation decided to lease the walls' defensive towers to some trades guilds to use as meeting houses.

Now follow the wall to the right and onto Bath Lane, so called because of the medical baths which were built here in 1781. They contained vapour baths and a large swimming pool but disappeared long ago.

On your left is another massive tower – **Durham Tower** – and a fine stretch of the restored town wall. At the foot of Bath Lane, on the left, the small 18th century building was once the meeting house for the Company of House Carpenters.

Across Westgate Road you can't miss the Journal Tyne Theatre. It opened as the Tyne Theatre in 1867 with Boucicault's *Arrah-na-Pogue*, considered by one contemporary reviewer as 'one of the most difficult of modern dramas to put upon the stage'. People queued for over two hours for tickets on opening night. Apparently the construction schedule had overrun (a problem shared by so many of today's cultural and leisure venues) and those in the queue were able to watch work still going on to complete the theatre. Eventually around 3,000 people took their seats in the auditorium. They were treated to a lengthy welcoming address by theatre manager, George Stanley, followed by a 112 line address in couplets, written by Mr Glynn and spoken by Miss Julia Desborough, before the play began.

Initially the Tyne Theatre was a real rival to the Theatre Royal, but by 1913 it was forced to add occasional moving pictures to its programme to attract audiences. The theatre closed on 1 March

Eilis O'Connell's 'Everchanging' and the Journal Tyne Theatre.

The Stoll cinema café, 1933.

1919 and opened again three months later as the Stoll cinema. It was a luxurious venue with a colour scheme of soft grey and cream tints with richly stencilled ornament. The draperies and seating were in a shade called rose du barri. The attendants at the dress circle entrance were young women dressed as highwaymen. There was also an elaborate winter garden café with a soda fountain in green onyx and a ladies' orchestra playing on the balcony. In 1929 the Stoll was the first cinema in Newcastle to show talking pictures.

A hidden theatrical treasure

The Stoll closed as a cinema in 1974 and eventually re-opened as a theatre. Theatre historians discovered that all the original Victorian stage machinery, including trap doors, was still intact. The machinery was restored to its original condition during the 1980s.

Walk past the theatre and cross Thornton Street. Set into the pavement is *Tyne Line of Text Flow* an artwork by Carol Sommer, Sue Downing and William Herbert, installed in 2005. The 140m long stream of text, in stainless steel, combines Roman messages found locally, printed text from the time of King Charles I and text messages collected in 2002 on the day of the Newcastle Sunderland football derby. They have been translated into SMS text form. William Herbert has written a response making reference to the Skinner Burn (another of Newcastle's hidden rivers) which flows under the street.

Now turn right into Pink Lane. The street takes its name from another of the towers on the Town Walls, Pink Tower, which stood at the junction of Pink Lane and Clayton Street, but was demolished in 1852. The Pink Tower was possibly named for the Pynke family.

On the south side of Clayton Street stands St Mary's Roman Catholic Cathedral. Designed by A.W.N. Pugin with pointed arches in a style reminiscent of 14th century architecture, St Mary's opened in 1844 and was granted cathedral status in 1850 (32 years before the Anglican St Nicholas' church became a cathedral). Funds raised for the construction of the church could not stretch to pay for the building of the tower and steeple, which were eventually added in 1872.

St Mary's stands on a triangular site. On the Neville Street side of the Cathedral is a statue of Cardinal Basil Hume, who was born in Ellison Place, Newcastle.

Opposite the third side of the Cathedral, near the bus stop on the east side of Bewick Street, a bronze relief of Thomas Bewick's Chillingham Bull is set into the pavement. This marks the approximate site of the house where the internationally-famous wood engraver lived between 1781 and

ST MARY'S CATHEDRAL.
NEWCASTLE ON TYNE.

Bewick's Chillingham Bull represented in bronze on Bewick Street.

1811. Born in 1753 at Cherryburn, near Mickley in Northumberland, Bewick was apprenticed at the age of 14 to Ralph Beilby, the Newcastle engraver. Bewick is most famous for his *General History of Quadrupeds* (1790) and his two volume *History of British Birds* (1797 and 1804), but many people today are familiar with his work without even realising it; it is used in advertising, packaging, newspaper and magazine illustration and even on T shirts and tea towels.

Continue down Bewick Street and cross Neville Street to the **Central Station**. The station was designed by John Dobson.

The unmistakable curve of Dobson's railway shed in 1860 and 140 years later. Look out for Victoria and Albert above the main exit.

The Stephenson Memorial in the 1880s.

Construction was begun in 1847 and the station was opened by Queen Victoria and Prince Albert in August 1850. Can you spot their medallions, along with that of Edward VII, inside the station, high up above the main exit? Dobson introduced many architectural innovations, including the use of curved iron principals in the roof, but some of the features of his original design (including an Italianate tower and porte-cocheres) were not built, saving more than £2,000 in construction costs. Look through the train shed for a spectacular view of the Castle Keep.

Near the Central Station, at the junction of Neville Street and Westgate Road, is the Stephenson Memorial, which was unveiled on 2 October 1862. Over 100,000 people attended the ceremony, which celebrated the genius of George Stephenson, father of modern railways. The figures at the base of the statue are a miner, a blacksmith, a platelayer and a locomotive engineer (although all seem rather

inappropriately dressed for their work), representing various facets of Stephenson's skills.

Walk past the Station Hotel, turn right and walk through the tunnel leading under the railway line. Look over the car park behind the Telegraph pub for a view of one of the best-preserved stretches of the town wall.

The huge statue outside Central Square (originally a 1930s post office building) is *Vulcan* by Sir Eduardo Paolozzi.

Now turn left onto South Street and walk past the post office sorting office until you reach **Stephenson's Works** at no. 20. On this site history was made and the

Courtesy Jeremy Beecham

An early drawing of Stephenson's Works.

world became a smaller place for ever. The unprepossessing building, dating from 1823, was the first purpose-built locomotive factory in the world. George Stephenson's son, Robert, then aged just 19, was managing partner. The pioneering designs *Rocket* and *Locomotion* were built here, and, as railways became a viable form of transport, locomotives produced in this factory were exported all over the world. Stephenson's Works closed in 1904, after the company moved to larger premises in Darlington,

Robert Stephenson 1803-1859

but engineering innovation continued on the site. George and Jobling, motor engineers, imported Ford chassis and built bespoke bodies for them here (one was the Golden Ford racing car). During the First World War the factory was used for the

The Stephenson's Works offices after restoration.

The Lit and Phil and Bolbec Hall, and
inset, the bust of an early patron,
Thomas Bewick inside the library.

(Lit & Phil)

construction of aircraft (probably Sopwith Camels). Contact the Robert Stephenson Trust on 0191 222 0905 for details of opening times.

Now retrace your steps back though the tunnel and turn right onto Westgate Road.

The extravagant Victorian Gothic sandstone building is Neville Hall, built in 1870 for the North of England Institute of Mining Engineers. Next door is the home of the **Literary and Philosophical Society** of Newcastle upon Tyne which dates from 1822. The Lit and Phil, as it is known locally, was founded in 1793 and met in a number of venues around the town, including the Groat Market, before moving to this Greek revival style building. The Society was never afraid of innovation, admitting women members by 1804, and hosting groundbreaking demonstrations of new technology. On October 20th 1880, during a lecture by Sir Joseph Swan (see page 40), the Society's lecture theatre was the first public room to be lit by electric light. By 1838, as well as a fine library, the Society owned a collection of scientific apparatus which members could enjoy either on the premises or, with the permission of the committee, in their own homes.

Next door is Bolbec Hall, built in 1907 by the Literary and Philosophical Society to attract an income from the letting out of rooms.

End your walk here, or retrace your steps to the Central Station to start the next walk.

The doorway of Bolbec Hall.

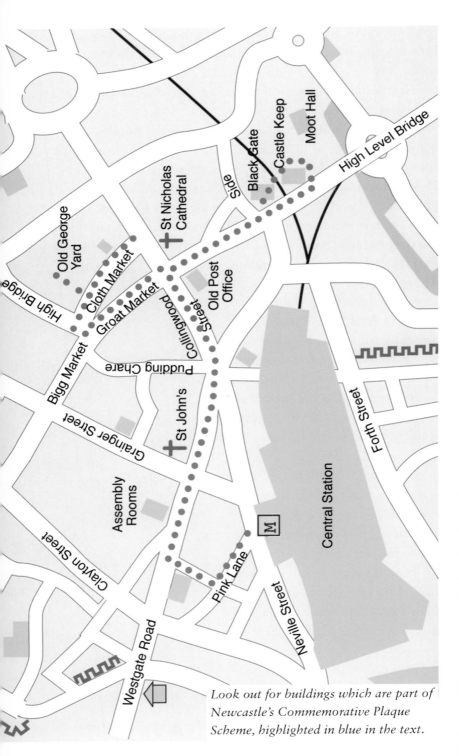

Look out for buildings which are part of Newcastle's Commemorative Plaque Scheme, highlighted in blue in the text.

Old George Yard

High Bridge

Cloth Market

Groat Market

St Nicholas Cathedral

Side

Black Gate

Castle Keep

Moot Hall

High Level Bridge

Old Post Office

Collingwood Street

Bigg Market

Pudding Chare

St John's

Grainger Street

Assembly Rooms

Central Station

Forth Street

Clayton Street

Pink Lane

Neville Street

M

Westgate Road

Castle and Cathedral

Start at the Central Station and cross Neville Street.

The artwork near the pedestrian crossing is *The Grainger Town Sculptural Map* by Tod Hanson and Simon Watkinson, installed in 2003. The map is a conceptual representation of Grainger Town, with buildings and landmarks reduced to their essential forms.

David Williams

This map of 1788 shows our path (and Bewick's) up Pink Lane, past Gunner Tower, and along Forth Lane to Westgate Road. Charlotte Street is now Fenkle Street, and the Central Station and Neville Street cover the Spital Field. The alley beside St John's will become Grainger Street. The Assembly Rooms are just opposite Forth Lane.

Now walk up Pink Lane (see page 65). Barely discernable behind the railings on the left are the remains of Gunner Tower, another of the defensive towers on the city walls (see page 61). Turn right down the lane between the Forth pub and the Jazz Café. This is the way that Thomas Bewick (see page 65) used to walk from his home to his workshop on Amen Corner. Look up to see the old window and the stone shield bearing the three castles from the Newcastle town arms above the tunnel that leads onto Westgate Road. This was once a town boundary stone (the boundary in this area was the town wall by Gunner Tower) which was moved here from an unknown location, possibly during the demolition of the Town Walls.

As you emerge from the alley, look at the Newcastle Arts Centre on your left. This low brick building dates from the mid to late 18th century and was once owned by University College Oxford. It was leased to wealthy Northumberland land owner, Sir Matthew White Ridley, who used it as a town house. Many of the buildings on this stretch of Westgate Road date from the same period and were used as town houses by the gentry. Look above the shop fronts to see examples of 18th century brick, stone and plasterwork.

At the junction is a statue of Joseph Cowen, (1829-1900) who was MP for Newcastle from 1873-1886. He also founded local newspaper, the *Newcastle Chronicle* in 1862 and the Tyne Theatre (see page 63) as well as smuggling arms to Italian Nationalist revolutionary, Giuseppe Garibaldi (see page 47).

The neo-classical stone building with Greek columns on the opposite side of the road is the Assembly Rooms. The building opened on 24 June 1766 as a meeting place for Newcastle's high society. In the early days up to 460 people could eat in the huge

supper room, they could play cards, dance, listen to concerts and make good marriages for their sons and daughters. In 1827 the Assembly Rooms hosted a ball to celebrate a visit of the Duke of Wellington to the town. Strauss gave a concert here on 20 October 1838 and provided music for a ball a month later. Franz Liszt gave a piano recital at the Assembly Rooms in 1841 and Charles Dickens and his theatrical company performed three playlets here in August 1852.

Entertainments at the Assembly Rooms

'How many brilliant companies have gathered in the spacious rooms, and how many happy hours have glided away to the magic sound of the gay dance music, since the good old time … when George the Third was king! Periwigs, powder and patches; full skirted coats, ample hoops and silver buckles have given way to other fashions and these, in their turn, have changed over and over again; yet still on occasion the black and grimy facade lightens up at the sight of the graceful forms which emerge from the carriages as they pause before the door, and the old rooms are still sometimes gay with music and dance.'

(From a newspaper article.)

Stay on the same side of the road as the Assembly Rooms and walk down hill towards Grainger Street. The house at no. 52

Westgate Road, **Gibb Chambers**, was built in 1861 for Charles John Gibb, the same Dr Gibb whose skills were promoted in the famous Geordie song *The Blaydon Races* (see also page 93).

Dr Charles John Gibb, 1824-1916, immortalised in 'The Blaydon Races'.

We flew past Armstrong's factory
And up by the Robin Adair
But gannin ower the Railway Bridge
The bus wheel flew off there
The lasses lost their crinolenes
And veils that hide their faces
I got two black eyes and a broken nose
In gannin to Blaydon races

Chorus:
Oh me lads, you should've seen us gannin
Passing the folks along the road
And all of them were starin'
All the lads and lasses there
They all had smilin' faces
Gannin along the Scotswood Road
To see the Blaydon races

Now when we got the wheel back on
Away we went again
But them that had their noses broke
They went back ower hyem
Some went to the dispensary
And some to Doctor Gibb's
And some to the infirmary
To mend their broken ribs

    Cross Grainger Street and head for St John's Church. Glance left at the flamboyant building, built in the style of a French chateau, with turrets, pavilions and balconies. Built between 1884 and 1887, this building looks like a fairytale castle, but its intended use was considerably more humdrum – it was designed as offices for the Newcastle and Gateshead Gas Company.

St John's, one of Newcastle's four original parish churches (see page 55), was probably founded in the 12th century but most of the building dates from the 14th and 15th centuries. In 1757 the funeral of a 14 year old boy, Thomas Matfield (sometimes recorded as Matfin) took place at the church. Thomas had been a

Sam Fairless

In 1860 St John's vicarage garden covered the area where the bottom of Grainger Street is today, extending to the Assembly Rooms.

pupil at St John's charity school and, as his coffin was brought into church, pupils from the school began to sing the funeral hymn. Then, to the horror of the pallbearers, something moved inside the coffin. The coffin was opened. Inside Thomas, dressed in a shroud, was beginning to stir, the shrill sound of the boy's voices having brought him out of a coma. He was rushed home, revived with a glass of cherry brandy and put to bed. He lived to the considerable age of 77, spending his working life as a keelman. He died in All Saint's poor house in 1820 and was finally laid to rest in All Saints churchyard.

Note the joke carved into the kerb stones (by artist Rupert Clamp) as the pavement curves around the churchyard: 'From here it is nine thousand, two hundred and fifty seven centimetres [how are you feeling?] to here'.

Further down Grainger Street, near the Junction with Westgate Road, is another public artwork, *Man with Potential Selves*, made by Sean Henry and installed in 2003. The piece comprises three views of the same man; one standing, one walking and one apparently floating horizontally above the ground. Each figure is 2.5m tall.

One of Sean Henry's realistic sculptures.

Turn left to rejoin Westgate Road, pass the entrance to Pudding Chare (the origins of the name of this old lane are lost to history, but one 19th century writer claimed that traders sold black puddings from stalls in this area) and along Collingwood Street (named for Admiral Lord Collingwood, the Newcastle-born hero of Trafalgar). It is full of financial institutions and is a magnificent monument to the Victorian money market.

On the right hand side of the road, the Allied Irish Bank

stands on the site of the old Turf Hotel, the centre of an infamous body-snatching scandal. An important coaching inn, the Turf received packages to be forwarded to all parts of the country. One Monday in September 1825, staff opening the booking office were overpowered by a foul stench. It was coming from a large box which had missed the last coach to Edinburgh on Saturday and had been stored in the office over the weekend.

Understandably suspicious, the staff called the constable who opened the box and discovered the body of a young woman. She appeared to have died from natural causes and, because there was no means of identifying her, was buried in a pauper's grave. In January of the following year, a huge box, weighing more than 16 stones, arrived at the Turf. Again, it was to be forwarded to an address in Edinburgh, the home of the great medical schools where the 'resurrectionists', Burke and Hare, made a not so

SUPERIOR TRAVELLING
FROM THE TURF HOTEL AND QUEEN'S HEAD,
NEWCASTLE-UPON-TYNE,
AND THE KING'S HEAD INN, DARLINGTON,
IN DIRECT CONNECTION WITH THE GREAT NORTH OF ENGLAND AND OTHER RAILWAYS.
COACHES LEAVE NEWCASTLE FOR DARLINGTON.

healthy living by supplying fresh corpses to doctors studying anatomy. Staff were immediately suspicious, the box was opened and the body of a man was discovered. Two more boxes containing corpses arrived at the Turf in 1828. One was delivered in person by an Edinburgh man named James Aitcheson. Although Aitcheson was questioned by police he was not arrested immediately and vanished from the town before further action could be taken. When Burke and Hare were tried for their crimes it emerged that Hare had spent some time in Newcastle in 1828. It is tempting to speculate that he was involved in some way with the grisly boxes at the Turf Hotel, and even that he could have been the mysterious James Aitcheson.

Collingwood Buildings, a hotel-turned-bank, with splendid arched windows, at the junction of Westgate Road and Collingwood Street, under construction in 1901.

The Keep in 1812.

At the end of Collingwood Street, cross the road and turn right, heading for the Castle Keep.

Newcastle takes its name from this 'new castle', founded in 1080 by Robert Curthose, son of William the Conqueror. This first, wooden, castle was a fortified enclosure, surrounded by a clay rampart, built on the site of a Roman fort (Pons Aelius) and an Anglo Saxon cemetery. For centuries Newcastle was a real frontier town and a vital part of the English defence against the Scots, so the castle was rebuilt in stone between 1168 and 1178. Some of the most advanced features of medieval engineering were incorporated into the building of the structure. The Keep's water supply comes into the building on the second floor. From there a system of lead pipes distributes it to lower parts of the Keep including the ground floor garrison room. If an enemy took the lower parts of the castle, the defenders could retreat to the upper floors, cutting off the water supply to the invaders. Offset windows meant that if, by some chance, an enemy arrow did fly through one of the narrow slit windows, it would hit a wall before it could too much damage.

As the political situation changed, the castle fell out of use, and by 1589 it was described as 'old and ruinous'. In 1643, however, the castle's defences had to be restored, and quickly, as Royalist Newcastle was besieged by the Scots army.

An offensive defence

As the Scots approached, mayor Sir John Marley had to find a way of shoring up Newcastle's defensive walls. Near the Keep was a huge dung heap, which in 1630 was noted to be a smelly 98 yards long, 10 yards high and 32 yards wide. It was removed by the resourceful mayor so ramparts could be built against the walls there. He also had cannons placed on the Keep.

The restored Castle Keep with
the characteristic battlements
which were added in 1810.
The cannon was to be fired from
the roof at noon each day but
this practice was soon stopped
because of damage to the
surrounding buildings!

The towering Castle Keep today. Still a brooding reminder of more turbulent times. (Paul MacDonald, Castle Keep)

After the Civil War, the castle once again fell into a state of disrepair. The chapel had become a beer cellar, the roof of the keep was a cabbage garden, houses (some of them four storeys high but only 10 feet wide) were packed into Castle Garth. The Black Gate (see below) was a tenement housing up to 60 people, and, at one point, a brothel. The guard room was a gaol. Prisoners awaiting trial (so not necessarily guilty) at the Assizes were kept here in appalling conditions. Prison reformer, John Howard, wrote: 'Men and women confined together for seven or eight nights … in a dirty damp dungeon … Having no roof, in wet season is some inches deep. The felons are chained to rings on the wall, shown to public like wild beasts and the vulgar and curious pay 6d each for admission'.

In 1810 the remains of the Castle Keep were bought by Newcastle Corporation who restored it over the next three years. The Keep is open to the public every day except Good Friday,

Christmas Day, Boxing Day and New Year's Day.

Walk around the Castle Keep anti-clockwise and through the railway viaduct. Here you can see excavated remains of other parts of the castle, including the infamous Heron Pit (named after William Heron, Sheriff of Northumberland and Keeper of the Castle from 1247 to his death in 1258) a dungeon with no doors or windows. Unfortunate prisoners were dropped into the pit through a trapdoor in the floor of the room above.

Now enter the passageway which takes you through the **Black Gate**, built between 1247 and 1250. You may be disappointed to know that the Black Gate is not called the Black Gate because it was the grim entrance to a terrible place, but simply because a Mr Patrick Black, a merchant from London, leased the building during the 17th century and lived there with his wife, Barbara.

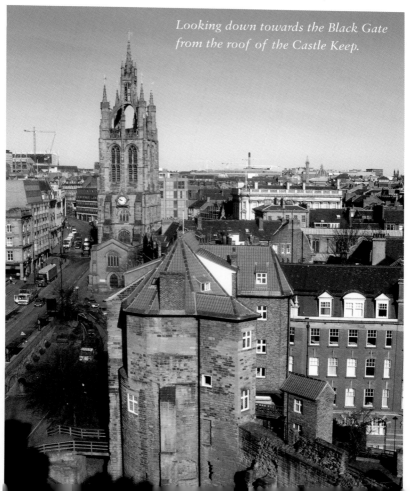

Looking down towards the Black Gate from the roof of the Castle Keep.

By the middle of the 19th century the Black Gate had become a slum accommodating twelve families and a public house. This photograph shows it in 1863. In 1883 the Society of Antiquaries took over the property and began repairs. They spent over £1,600 on improvements.

For over a hundred years the Black Gate has been the residence of the Society of Antiquaries of Newcastle upon Tyne, the oldest antiquarian society in the world outside London and Edinburgh.

Turn right as you leave the Black Gate and pass the entrance of the steep, twisting street called Side (possibly because it runs down the side of a hill). Until the 1780s this used to be one of two steep routes from the river to the higher parts of town. In wet or icy conditions it could be a hazard to horses, carts, carriages and other forms of conveyance.

On 26 September, 1748, a boy called **Cuthbert Collingwood** was born to a poor but respectable family in a house near the top of the Side. The site of his birthplace is marked by his bust above a doorway of the Edwardian Milburn House. At the age of 13, young Cuthbert went to sea to be trained to be a naval officer. In 1773 he met Horatio Nelson who recognised Collingwood's talents and recommended him to Sir Peter Parker. Collingwood was promoted to Post Captain and he and Nelson became lifelong friends. Collingwood's skills as a naval commander were demonstrated during the war against France which began in 1793. At the Battle of Trafalgar (1805), his ship was first to fire and first to be fired on. After the death of Nelson and the British victory, a terrible storm blew up. Collingwood's action saved the British fleet from destruction. Collingwood was made Commander-in-Chief of the Mediterranean. He died in 1810.

Walk towards St Nicholas' Cathedral. You will pass **Amen Corner** where Ralph Beilby and Thomas Bewick had their workshop. The site of

Cuthbert Collingwood (top), Thomas Bewick, and a rather strange rabbit all live on nearby buildings.

a later workshop is marked by a bust of Bewick set above a doorway at the far corner. See if you can spot the strange rabbit over the door of one of the buildings behind the Cathedral.

St Nicholas' was one of Newcastle's four original parish churches and was made a cathedral in 1882. Although some of the architecture dates from the 12th and 13th centuries, the majority belongs to the 14th and 15th centuries. The structure is dominated by a magnificent 'Scottish Crown' tower, dating from around 1470.

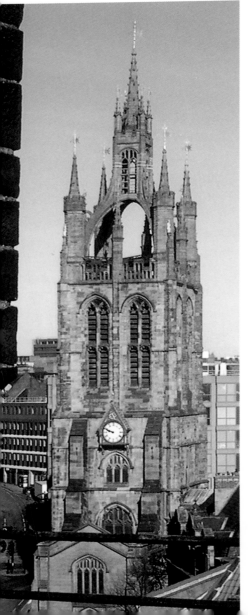

Not everyone has appreciated the design of the tower. T. Sopwith, in his 1838 Stranger's *Pocket Guide to Newcastle upon Tyne and its Environs* quotes Dr Dibdin in his *Northern Tour*:

'The tower of the Church of St Nicholas strikes me as being one of the heaviest, coarsest and most stunted church towers in the kingdom. There is nothing ecclesiastical about it. And then for the ornaments, or cap, upon the summit, these appear to me to be decidedly objectionable on two grounds; the one, that the whole additions are disproportionately short or compressed, the other that it does not belong to what it is fixed upon.'

Mr Sopwith is rather indignant about Dr Dibdin's harsh criticism and quotes Sir James Hall's essay on Gothic architecture, in which he describes the tower as 'One of the boldest and most beautiful works in this or any other style.'

Opposite the Cathedral, on the other side of St Nicholas Street, is the old General Post Office building. Opened on 25 April, 1876, to replace an outdated office on the quayside, the new building made possible a startling innovation -- the employment of women. A contemporary report on the opening of the new Post Office revealed:

'At present no ladies are employed at the Newcastle Post-office, although the employment of female telegraph clerks for sometime now has been largely practised in the south. Hitherto there has not been proper accommodation for ladies in the Newcastle Post Office; hence the fact that they have not been employed. However, now that ample provision has been obtained for all requirements, those who desire situations of the sort may

The Post Office around 1900. Ladies could be employed there at last.

ere long hope to be engaged as telegraph clerks in Newcastle. The male officials will enter the premises by a door at the back of the premises. The ladies will be admitted through a door to the north of the portico and will ascend two flights of stairs, by which they will reach their retiring room, thence the instrument room.'

Cross Mosley Street and walk up Groat Market. Groats (oats with the husks removed) were once an important food for both humans and animals.

On the left is the Blackie Boy pub (previously the Black Boy Inn), which is one of the oldest pubs in Newcastle. In 1829 it was advertised for sale with desirable features including stabling, malt kiln, brewing apparatus, a pump of excellent water in the yard and a long room where 200 people could eat. In 1889 the rear of the premises collapsed, so what you see now is a rebuild dating from 1890.

During the 18th century, the Blackie Boy was home to a club, known as Swarley's Club, after the inn's landlord Richard Swarley. Its most famous member was the engraver, Thomas Bewick. Bewick described his fellow members as merchants or respectable tradesmen and said that the club had few rules, except that every member should behave as a gentleman. Anyone who transgressed was fined, and if the fine was not paid the member in question was dismissed from the club.

A very different sort of club met at the Flying Horse, an inn which once stood on the site of ncjMedia (home of Newcastle's daily newspapers). By and large the pub had a respectable clientele, but one of its rooms was known locally as Hell's Kitchen. This was the haunt of the town's low life, including Euphy Scott, queen of the fishwives, Owld Judy, guardian of the town hutch (the wooden chest where the town's revenues were kept), and Blind Willie Purvis, a writer of popular songs. Landlord, Ralph Nicholson, was taking no chances with these characters. The poker by the fire was four feet long and might have made a handy weapon had not Nicholson chained it to the fireplace. If an argument broke out Nicholson would lock the doors and stop anyone leaving until peace was restored. Persistent troublemakers were banned from the inn for six months.

The Blackie Boy is on the right of this view down the Groat Market towards the cathedral. The painting is 'The Lost Child' by James Ramsay (1786-1854) and features a portrait of Thomas Bewick in the top hat to the left. The town bellman is announcing the loss of a child, but in the distance we see the child has been found safe and sound.

Continue up the hill until you reach Bigg Market (bigg is another type of grain; a species of barley), and cross over to the Half Moon Chambers. There has been a Half Moon on this site since around 1550. In 1830 it was a coaching inn, and here travellers waited for coaches named the True Briton, the Phoenix or the Adventurer to take them to destinations such as Durham, Morpeth, Bedlington and Hexham. The present building dates from 1902-1905 and was designed by the same architects responsible for Emerson Chambers on Blackett Street. Note the dormer windows shaped like witches' hats and the half moon symbols on the balconies.

Now walk down Cloth Market (which runs parallel to Groat

Market). An arch on your left leads to the Old George Inn and Yard. The inn dates from the 17th century (perhaps even earlier) but was altered during the 18th and 19th centuries. According to tradition, Charles I, during his captivity in Newcastle (see page 40), was allowed to play 'goff' (golf) at Shieldfield and, on his return, stop off at the Old George for a drink.

Old George Yard has all the feel of a 17th century coaching inn. There was once a horse ramp to first floor stables.

Below, the inn in 1924.

Towards the bottom of Cloth Market is **Balmbra's**, a pub made famous by the song *The Blaydon Races* by George Ridley (we encountered this song on page 77). The song was introduced on 4 June 1862 at a grand concert in aid of Harry Clasper, a champion oarsman. It was organised by John Balmbra, landlord of the pub, which was then known as the Wheatsheaf.

I went to Blaydon Races
'Twas on the 9th of June
Eighteen Hundred and Sixty Two
On a summer's afternoon
I took the bus from Balmbra's
And she was heavy laden
Away we went along Collingwood Street
To see the Blaydon Races

Cross Mosley Street to the statue of Queen Victoria beside St Nicholas' Cathedral. It was sculpted by Alfred Gilbert and unveiled in 1903. She faces Collingwood Street and the Central Station because it was felt that Her Majesty could not turn her back on the church. Queen Victoria had no particular love for Newcastle, and she is said to have ordered the blinds on her carriage to be lowered every time she passed through. Various

reasons have been suggested for her dislike of the place; they range from a dispute with the Royal Station Hotel over a bill to her horror at the republican sentiments expressed by some of the townsfolk, notably Joseph Cowen (see page 75).

The site on which Queen Victoria's statue stands is said to be a burial ground for cholera victims.

End your walk here, or retrace your steps along Cloth Market to the Beehive Hotel to the next walk.

Sam Fairless

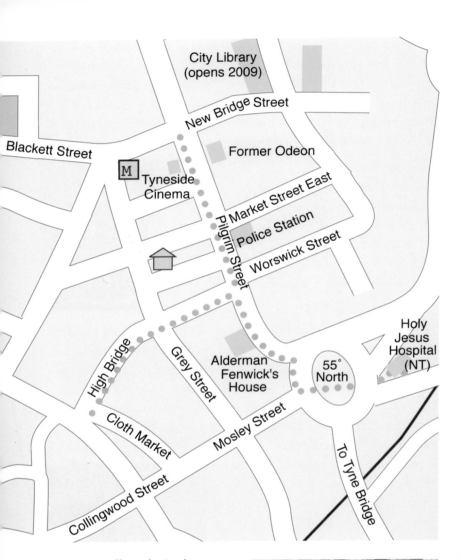

City Library
(opens 2009)

New Bridge Street

Blackett Street

Former Odeon

M

Tyneside
Cinema

Market Street East

Pilgrim Street

Police Station

Worswick Street

High Bridge

Grey Street

Alderman
Fenwick's
House

55°
North

Holy
Jesus
Hospital
(NT)

Cloth Market

Mosley Street

Collingwood Street

To Tyne Bridge

*Start your walk at the Beehive
Hotel at the corner of Cloth
Market and High Bridge.
There has been at least one other
Beehive on this site, but the present
building dates from 1902. Take a
look up at its copper domed tower
and admire the colourful tiles at the
door.*

Pilgrims and Friars

Start your walk at the Beehive Hotel on the corner of Cloth Market and High Bridge.

High Bridge crosses another of Newcastle's hidden streams, the Lort Burn, and until 1785 when the river was culverted, was the only route between the market area of Newcastle and Pilgrim Street. High Bridge also gives us an idea of the way Newcastle streets looked before Grainger's redevelopment of the town. Although many of the buildings on High Bridge date from the 19th century, the irregular plot sizes and the twisting, narrow street date from a much earlier period than the neat wide streets of Grainger's era.

In 1878 the landlord of the Duke of Wellington was William Campbell, famous for being the heaviest man in the country at a colossal 53 stones. When he died that year, aged just 22, his huge lead-lined coffin had to be extracted from a third floor window of the pub by a special winch. A crowd 40,000 strong is said to have watched the funeral procession on its way to Jesmond Cemetery. He was obviously a popular man!

Above, William Campbell. Right, the medieval twist of High Bridge. The Duke of Wellington is on the left, and the Beehive Hotel at the far end.

Cross Grey Street and continue along High Bridge. In 2006 archaeologists discovered the remains of a Bronze Age roundhouse, nearly 3,500 years old, near the Bacchus pub. It is the earliest evidence of settlement in the Newcastle area and probably would have formed part of a community with several other houses.

The excavations also revealed the wall of a house and yard, dating from the late 12th to early 13th century, on the corner of High Bridge and Pilgrim Street. Investigation of the rubbish dump and latrines showed that the diet of people living here included hazel nuts, haws, plums, sloes, rosehips, blackberries, raspberries, elderberries, strawberries, cereals and meat. The archaeologists discovered that a three-room extension had been added to the medieval house in the 14th century. Evidence of

Pilgrim Street is central in this 1745 engraving by Nathaniel Buck.

metalworking suggests that items produced here could have been sold in a shop in the part of the building fronting onto Pilgrim Street.

Turn right onto Pilgrim Street. This ancient street probably dates from the end of the 12th century, and it appears in records under its present name from the mid-13th century. It is often said that Pilgrim Street indicates the route pilgrims would take to St Mary's Chapel at Jesmond or to the relics of St Francis of Assisi belonging to the Grey Friars (in the present Blackett Street area), but there is no evidence for this. The latest research tells us that 'pilgrim' (Latin 'peregrinorum') signifies travellers or foreigners – so we are in the street of the foreigners' quarter. William Grey, writing in 1649, described it as 'the longest and fairest street in the town'.

By 1910 this once select street was mostly run down tenements.

The story of a Newcastle house 🔑

The oldest building still standing on Pilgrim Street is 'Alderman Fenwick's House', a 17th century dwelling built on the site of St Cuthbert's Inn which was a medieval hostelry.

The house was probably built in around 1660. The first known owner, Thomas Winship, a member of the Tanner's company who died in 1695, left it to his daughter Sarah in his will. Sarah married Nicholas Fenwick who made extensive alterations to the house. From the mid 17th century to mid 18th century the Northumbrian Fenwick family were prominent merchants and were also involved in local politics as aldermen, sheriffs and mayors. Because the name Nicholas was used for so many Fenwick boys nobody can be sure for which one the house was named but it seems likely that it was for Nicholas Fenwick, baptised in 1692, and nephew of Sarah's husband Nicholas, who died in 1725. Sarah died in 1733.

In 1781 the house was bought by Charles Turner, landlord of the Queen's Head Hotel further down Pilgrim Street. Charles transferred his business and the inn's name to his new house and his former property became known as the Old Queen's Head.

Alderman Fenwick's house remained the Queen's Head Inn

The Queen's Head advertises in 1855. It backed on to Grey Street.

The restored Alderman Fenwick's House, Pilgrim Street.

for over a century. It was a coaching inn with 35 main rooms and was also used for receptions, banquets and auction sales.

On January 28, 1828, a mysterious long box was delivered to the coaching inn by a man with a soft Scottish accent. Aware of the gruesome discoveries at the Turf Hotel (see page 80) staff were immediately suspicious and opened the box. They were horrified to discover the body of a child, Lizzie Mills, a shoemaker's daughter who had been buried at Byker earlier in the week. Police were called and they rushed to the graveyard to discover very few signs of disturbance at the little girl's grave. The bodysnatchers were so skilful that, had it not been for the suspicions of the Queen's Head staff, the taking of Lizzie's body could have gone unnoticed.

In 1883 the house underwent another change of use when it was leased to the Newcastle upon Tyne Liberal Club. Alterations to the premises included the provision of a library, two smoking rooms, one of which was affectionately known as 'The Slump', a first-floor library extending the whole width of the building, two 'tete-a-tete' rooms for conversation or confidences of members, a chess room and a billiard room with raised benches for spectators. There were seven bedrooms for members wishing to stay in town overnight.

Two world wars, changes on the political scene and a decline in membership left the Liberal Club in a poor financial situation. In 1959 parts of the upper floors were boarded up to reduce the rates bill. In 1962 it was decided that the club should vacate the building. Alderman Fenwick's House stood empty, and rapidly deteriorating until 1982, when the City Council invited the Tyne and Wear Building Preservation Trust to restore the building. The aim of the restoration project was to repair the existing fabric of the building using traditional techniques and materials. The final phase of the project was completed in 1997.

Continue down Pilgrim Street and cross to the 55° North building via the crossing at the corner of Mosley Street.

The beautifully restored cupola and windvane, and right, the house in the 1720s. You can just see the cupola from across the road.

A detail of 'The Royal Arcade' by John Dobson and J.W. Carmichael.
(Tyne & Wear Museums)

A grandiose failure

The bar at 55° North contains the remnants of a replica of the interior of the Royal Arcade, a sumptuous development of shops and offices, designed by John Dobson and completed in 1832 (though you will have to ask if you want to see it). In its time it was considered to be the finest arcade in the country. The interior was a splendid avenue 250 feet long, 20 feet wide, with shops on either side, lit by 8 conical skylights and floored with chequered stone and black marble. But it never really caught on. Arcade developments that attracted the maximum number of shoppers were U-shaped or led from one thriving shopping street to another. The Royal Arcade fronted onto fashionable Pilgrim Street, but the rear entrance led to Manor Chare, not the most salubrious of areas, and one where well-to-do consumers had no reason to go. In 1841 some shop were still unlet, and by 1880 the area had become even more run down. Demolition was proposed but the building survived, in an increasingly dilapidated condition, until the 1960s when it was removed to make way for Swan House, the office complex that is now 55° North. The Royal Arcade was taken down stone by stone with the intention of rebuilding it on a nearby site. This never happened and, over time, even the stones of England's finest arcade were lost.

Walk round to the back of the 55° North complex and look over the road to the gable end of the General Soup Kitchen and Holy Jesus Hospital. Now follow the subway until you reach the building itself.

As far as we know, the first building on this site was a friary, dating from around 1291. It was built by the black-robed Augustinian (or Austin) friars. As well as a church and cloister, there was accommodation for around 25 friars, a guest house for travellers, gardens and outbuildings.

The friars' occupation of the site came to an end with the dissolution of the monasteries. From 1539, the friary was used as a meeting place and residence for Henry VIII's Council of the North, a body set up to administer the region north of the Yorkshire border. Soon the former friary became known as King's Manor; this area is still called Manors today. The tower (now at the rear of the Holy Jesus Hospital building) was built in the late 16th century to house soldiers, munitions and armour. By the end of the 18th century the ground floor of the tower was used to imprison drunks and other disorderly townsfolk.

The next phase of the development was the Holy Jesus Hospital, opened in 1682. It was designed to house 42 retired Freemen of the town, their widows or unmarried dependent children. Each resident had their own small room with a fireplace and its own front door. The doors leading to the ground floor rooms can still be seen today. The only water was supplied by the Pant, which was moved from the hospital's garden to its present site at the front of the building in 1882 when City Road was built.

Every year residents were given a new suit of clothes, coal and a small amount of money. There was, however a price to pay for this comfort and security. The hospital was governed by a Master and two Sisters who enforced strict rules for the discipline of residents. Residents had to attend church every Sunday, they were locked in their rooms from 9pm until 6am, and drunkenness was banned.

Holy Jesus Hospital continued to be used until 1935, when residents were moved to bungalows in Spital Tongues.

Holy Jesus Hospital before the pant was moved in 1882. Otherwise the exterior has changed little since then.

In 1880 a soup kitchen was built onto the side of Holy Jesus Hospital. The aim was to provide cheap, nourishing food for Newcastle's deserving poor. To qualify to buy soup, people had to apply to the subscribers of the soup kitchen or the local parish. Drinkers, the immoral and able-bodied men considered capable of work were excluded at this stage. Soup (up to 800 pints at a time) was only supplied on 'officially' cold days (as decided by the committee). Ticket holders queued with their own jugs or jars to buy soup at a penny per pint.

The recipe for the soup came from the governor of the nearby Carliol Square gaol. In the summer, when the kitchen was not needed for soup production, female ex-convicts were employed to wash prison laundry in the soup boilers.

The soup kitchen closed in 1891 when committee members discovered that some ticket holders were buying soup and reselling it at a profit to Newcastle's lodging houses.

By the early 20th century the Manors area was becoming increasingly industrialised. A brass foundry occupied the tower and in 1913 the soup kitchen building was converted into a chemical factory. This must have made living conditions very unpleasant for the residents of the hospital.

In 1971, the restored Holy Jesus Hospital, tower and soup kitchen reopened as the John George Joicey Museum. The displays were relocated to The Discovery Museum in 1993, and the National Trust's Inner City Project moved into the building in

Holy Jesus Hospital in 1935. The building is now tucked up against the Central Motorway.

2000. There is limited public access to the building at certain times; for details call 0191 255 7610.

Now retrace your steps to the east side of Pilgrim Street. The building on the corner of Pilgrim Street and Worswick Street was erected in 1899 and has a carved head above each of the 22 first storey windows. As well as bearded 19th century men, they include an African boy and an Egyptian Pharaoh. These heads have always been the subject of some speculation. Who or what do they represent? In 1961 a journalist wrote an article on the heads, suggesting that they were usually held to represent heroes such as General Gordon. Subsequently a reader wrote to the paper to describe her meeting with the sculptor of the heads, J. Rodgers, when he was an old man. He told her 'when I was asked to sculpt the heads on Pilgrim and Worswick Streets, I thought for a very long time and then had a brain wave. I brought out our family album of photographs. Then the work started and they represented a few aunts and uncles of mine.'

Pilgrim Street around 1906. Above the Royal Arcade the street became more impressive with large new buildings on either side of the road.

To the right of the tram standard in the middle of the road is the old Central Police Station which was replaced in the 1930s. Before the opening of the Tyne Bridge in 1928 traffic was light, but that would change as Pilgrim Street became the main route to the north.

CASTLE.

Between Worswick Street and Market Street is the combined fire station, police station and courts building. Can you spot the griffins at each side of the upper windows on the Pilgrim Street and Market Street fascias? According to the programme for the official opening of the building on 16 June 1933, these mythical creatures suggest 'Power, Watchfulness and Swiftness to act, qualities equally appropriate to the operation of the Law as to the duties of the Fire Brigade.'

The large white art deco building on the opposite corner of Market Street is Carliol House, built between 1924 and 1928 as headquarters for the Newcastle upon Tyne Electric Supply Company. At the time electricity was an exciting innovation in domestic power supply, and Carliol House, with its high-speed electric lifts and electrically powered central heating, was designed to be a showcase for the most up-to-the minute technology.

Carliol House and the Pilgrim Street Police Station. The fire station is now disused.

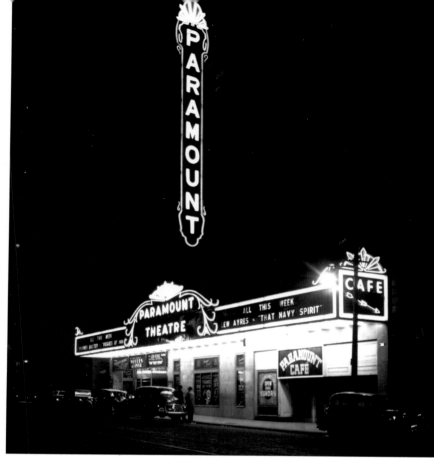

The Paramount in its super-cinema heyday, 1938.

Further along the block is a disused cinema that was once the pride of the city. Opened in 1931 as the Paramount (it later became an Odeon), it boasted almost double the seating capacity (2,602) of any other cinema in Newcastle and was intended to provide the ultimate in luxury. With light fittings finished in 9-carat gold, fresh flowers in the foyer, a 'daintily furnished' ladies' cosmetic room and usherettes daringly dressed in 'trousers of French grey', a visit to this cinema was truly special. A contemporary report describes the auditorium ceiling as 'fancifully resembling a night sky upon which gilded designs are seen on a dark ground … The walls are divided into

panels by pilasters which 'flower' into glass illumination fittings behind which … coloured lamps in amber, blue and red create a very dainty result. Above them graceful figures in metal enhance the general effect. The panels between the pilasters are of silk, painted with figures suggesting Watteau, the colours being rich and blending with the general scheme.'

The building cost £250,000, not all of which was spent on cosmetic enhancements. The cinema boasted the latest technology including sound by Western Electric and, of course, a mighty deluxe Wurlitzer organ.

On the opposite side of Pilgrim Street, at the corner of the narrow High Friar Lane is a much more modest cinema. Conceived and designed by Dixon Scott (great uncle of Hollywood director Ridley Scott), it was opened as the News Theatre in 1937. The idea was that shoppers with an hour or so to spare before catching a bus or train could watch a continuous programme of news reels, cartoons and special sport and travel features. Originally the cinema was reached from Pilgrim Street, through an arcade with a mosaic

The Tyneside Cinema and High Friar Lane 1971.

and terrazzo floor, marble walls and 'delicate mouldings and paintings … executed in ancient Persian designs.' The pay-box was a creation of marble, granite and stainless steel. In contrast to the opulent entrance, the auditorium was almost stark in its simplicity.

Cinema news reels couldn't complete with television news bulletins and the News Theatre closed in 1968. The building was taken over by the Tyneside Film Theatre and now operates as the Tyneside Cinema. At the time of writing the Pilgrim Street building is closed while the interior (including the spectacular mosaics) is restored to its former art deco glory.

The lane is High Friar Lane, another reminder that this area was once dominated by a religious house, and incidentally, the street where Richard Grainger was born. The walk ends here, although if you continue a little further up Northumberland Street and turn right towards Princess Square you can check on the progress of Newcastle's new City Library, a magnificent 21st century building designed as a backdrop and showcase for a treasure trove of resources including an unrivalled local and family history collection.

An impression of Newcastle's new City Library, due to open in 2009, from Blue Carpet Square. (Kajima Partnerships Ltd.)

Useful information

Visitor Information Centres are situated on Market Street (next to Central Arcade) and at the Guildhall on Newcastle Quayside. Contact them for all information on heritage events, tours, accommodation and much more.
Telephone 0191 2778000; www.newcastle.gov.uk

Blackfriars Restaurant & Meeting Rooms holds a wide range of events throughout the year including medieval banquets.
Telephone 0191 2615945; www.blackfriarsrestaurant.co.uk

Holy Jesus Hospital telephone 0191 255 7610

Castle Keep telephone 0191 232 7938; www..newcastle.ac.uk/keep

Robert Stephenson Trust telephone 0191 222 0905
www.robertstephensontrust.com

For a wide range of informative illustrated books on Tyneside visit www.tynebridgepublishing.co.uk

Extend your walk to the Quayside with *Unlocking the Quayside* by Vanessa Histon, available from Tyne Bridge Publishing.

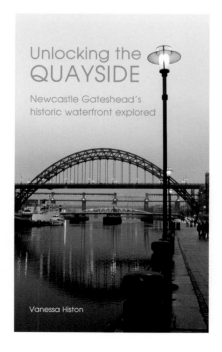